HEY, PEANUTS!

Selected Cartoons From
MORE PEANUTS
Vol. 2

by Charles M. Schulz

A Fawcett Crest Book

Fawcett Publications, Inc., Greenwich, Conn.

Member of American Book Publishers Council, Inc.

Other PEANUTS Books in Fawcett Crest Editions:

This book, prepared especially for Fawcett Publications, Inc., comprises the second half of MORE PEANUTS, and is reprinted by arrangement with Holt, Rinehart and Winston, Inc.

Eighteenth Fawcett Crest printing October 1969

Published by Fawcett World Library, 67 West 44th Street, New York, N. Y. 10036 Printed in the United States of America

BOY, AM I EVER DEPRESSED
SOMEBODY ELSE IS DEPRESSED TOO, I SEE
THAT'S THE ONLY THING THAT COULD POSSIBLY HAVE CHEERED ME UP!
SCHULZ

SCHULZ